Who's Who at the Zoo?

by Francisco León
illustrated by Beth Buffington

Orlando Boston Dallas Chicago San Diego

This tiger has room to roam at the zoo, but it is not running loose. What other animals live at the zoo?

Baboons live at the zoo. In the wild, they live in herds called troops. Baboons eat foods such as shoots of plants, eggs, and insects.

A moose lives at this zoo. Moose are tall. They have to stoop down, or kneel, to drink from a shallow pool of water!

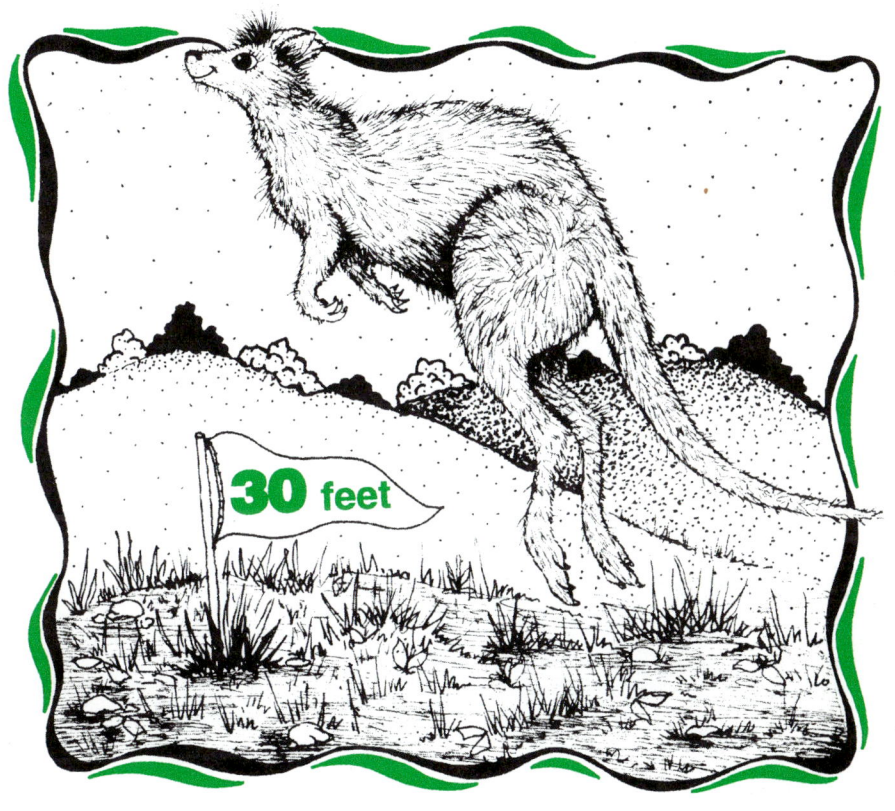

Here are the kangaroos. They have strong back legs and a strong tail to use as tools when they leap. Kangaroos can leap 30 feet!

Big black-and-white pandas eat bamboo. Black-and-white pandas eat the bamboo shoots, the stems, and the leaves, too.

Red pandas eat bamboo leaves. Some people think red pandas are a lot like raccoons. Both have tails with rings on them.

Can a raccoon be a dog? No, but there is a raccoon dog. It is a kind of fox, that has a mask on its face like a raccoon.

You might think that the anteater is in a gloomy mood. It is not. It just looks gloomy because its nose is so long that it droops!

You will not see one tooth in an anteater's mouth. Anteaters don't have teeth. How do you think they eat their food?

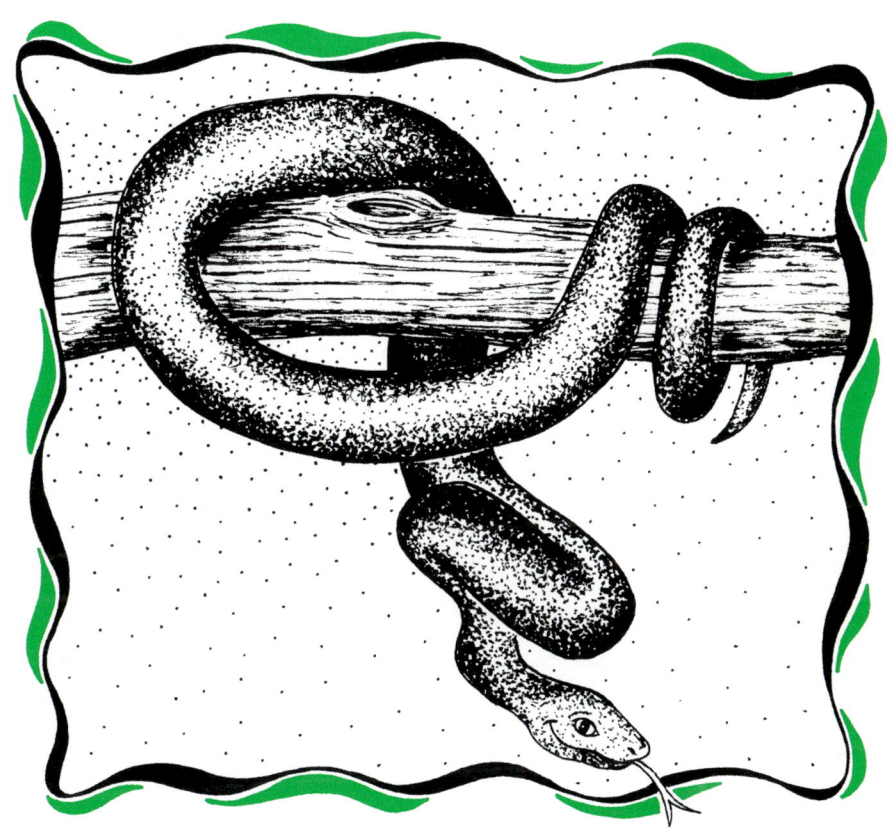

Snakes live in the reptile rooms. People used to think that the mud snake could form a loop and roll like a hoop. It can't!

Seals stay cool in their pool. They swim smoothly under the water. Soon it will be noon. Then the zookeeper will give them food.

Many birds live at the zoo. This is a spoonbill. Does its bill look like a spoon? You could scoop up a lot of food with a spoon that big!

Coots live in this zoo, too. Coots can't take off from land. They zoom on the water until they are running so fast that they can fly!

Loons are diving birds that swoop down into the water to catch food. Loons' nests are so close to the water that they can slide right in!

A lot of animals live in the zoo. They need room to roam and food to eat. What a lot of work a zookeeper's job must be!